The
Southern Railway
Story

Inevitably, in writing a book such as this, I am indebted to the National Railway Museum at York and the vast treasure trove of information contained in its search engine about the old railway companies, their trains and rolling stock, and the people who worked for them. I am also grateful to Sophia Brothers of the Science & Society Picture Library. Those in the distant past who compiled and wrote for the *Southern Railway Magazine* also did much to shed light on the workings of the railway.

The smallest of the so-called Big Four (the grouped railway companies), the Southern differed by being the least dependent on freight traffic. It lagged behind the other companies in introducing powerful steam locomotives and did not receive its first 4-6-2 Pacific steam locomotives until the Second World War. But it was far ahead of the others when it came to electrification, completing first the inner suburban electrification and then the outer suburban electrification by 1929, after which it headed for the coast. By the outbreak of the Second World War in 1939, the main lines as far west as Portsmouth and as far east as Eastbourne were electrified, and Hastings could be reached from London by electric train, but only on the indirect route via Eastbourne.

CONTENTS

Published in the United Kingdom in 2013 by
The History Press
The Mill · Brimscombe Port · Stroud · Gloucestershire · GL5 2QG

British Library Cataloguing in Publication Data
A catalogue record for this book is available from the British
Library.

Hardback ISBN 978-0-7524-8804-2

Typesetting and origination by The History Press
Printed in India

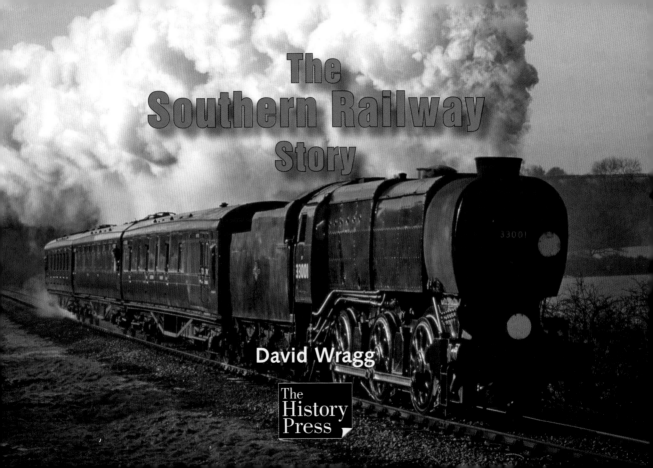

While not renowned for its expresses, with nothing to match the prestigious expresses of its three peer companies, the Southern did have the notable 'Golden Arrow' boat train and the 'Atlantic Coast Express', which served much of north Devon and north Cornwall. Its 'Brighton Belle' was the world's first electric multiple unit Pullman train. Perhaps most significant of all, but now largely overlooked, was the 'Night Ferry', the only sleeping car service on the Southern, which used wagons-lits suitably scaled down to meet the much tighter British loading gauge, and provided a through service each night between London and Paris without changing.

The Southern had more London termini than any of the other companies, with no less than seven, while the largest, Waterloo, had been rebuilt by the London & South Western Railway to become the first terminus designed for the electric train. The Southern had the only tube railway in London not operated by the Underground Group or its successor, the London Passenger Transport Board, in the Waterloo and City Line, linking Waterloo with the City of London.

It may not have been the largest or fastest of Britain's railways, but it was a great railway and remarkably forward-looking.

The Railways Act 1921 enforced the grouping of more than a hundred railway companies into four big concerns, one of which was described in the Act as the 'Southern Group of Companies'. A whole year, 1922, was allowed for the new companies to establish themselves and make managerial appointments. The new Southern Railway took over the operations and assets of three substantial companies and many smaller ones. Under the Act, the larger companies were known as constituent companies and were able to appoint directors to the board of the Southern Railway, while the smaller companies were described as subsidiary companies.

The Southern had three constituent companies which were the London & South Western Railway (LSWR); the London Brighton & South Coast Railway (LB&SCR) and the South Eastern & Chatham Railway Companies Managing Committee, which managed two impoverished companies, the South Eastern Railway (SER) and the London Chatham & Dover Railway (LC&DR). The LSWR and LB&SCR actually collaborated in the Portsmouth area and on the Isle of Wight, jointly managing the line between Havant and Portsmouth Harbour, the ferry service from Portsmouth to Ryde, and the railway line between Ryde Pier Head and Smallbrook Junction, where the lines of the Isle of Wight Railway and the Isle of Wight Central Railway diverged, although neither of the two mainland companies ran any trains on the island.

The list of subsidiary companies was long. There were no less than three companies on the Isle of Wight. The Isle of Wight Railway

◀ The largest of the Southern's predecessor companies and the one with the longest services, stretching into Devon and north Cornwall, was the London & South Western Railway (LSWR). This was one of the company's smaller locomotives, an 'M7' class tank locomotive, preserved in British Railways livery. (Cody Images)

was the busiest with a line connecting Ryde, a busy resort and the main ferry port, with the other popular resorts of Sandown, Shanklin and Ventnor. There was also the Isle of Wight Central Railway, linking Ryde with Newport and Cowes, as well as having a line between Newport and Sandown with a branch to Ventnor West. The third company

in this trio was the Freshwater, Yarmouth & Newport (Isle of Wight) Railway Company, with just three locomotives.

The other companies were the Bridgwater Railway Company; Brighton & Dyke Railway Company; Hayling Railway Company; Lee-on-Solent Railway Company; London & Greenwich Railway Company; Mid Kent Railway Company; North Cornwall Railway Company; Plymouth & Dartmoor Railway Company; Plymouth, Devonport & South Western Junction Railway Company; Sidmouth Railway Company; and the Victoria Station & Pimlico Railway Company.

The Plymouth, Devonport & South Western Junction Railway Company had

Did You Know?

While the old LSWR had been the largest of the companies merged to form the Southern Railway, it was not the smartest. That accolade belonged to the LB&SCR, which with the GWR and the Midland Railway had a reputation for comfortable trains, at least for first-class passengers.

◄◄ The weakest of the mainland companies absorbed into the Southern Railway was the South Eastern & Chatham (SECR), itself a management company to coordinate the London Chatham & Dover Railway and the South Eastern Railway. This is the former SECR 0-6-0 'C' class locomotive preserved on the Bluebell Railway in Sussex. (Cody Images)

◄ Amongst the locomotives and rolling stock inherited from the predecessor companies was this J2 locomotive, seen at London Bridge with ex-SECR 'birdcage' brake. Powerful tank engines such as this were ideal for many pre-electrification suburban journeys. (HMRS)

▲ Of the Southern's predecessor companies, the London, Brighton & South Coast had the most 'upmarket' image, but it also had the highest proportion of tank engines. This is a former LB&SCR 55 *Stepney*, a 0-6-0T A1 Terrier class, preserved on the Bluebell Line in Sussex. (Cody Images)

▲ This former LB&SCR 0-6-0T was sold to the much less affluent Isle of Wight Central Railway and then passed into Southern hands. It is now preserved on the Isle of Wight Steam Railway, where it is on what would have been IWCR tracks. (Cody Images)

already been acquired by the LSWR, which had used its line to reach Plymouth once it opened in 1890, freeing the LSWR from having to use the south Devon route of its rival, the Great Western (GWR), for London to Plymouth traffic. While not covered by the Act, the Lynton & Barnstaple Railway, with a 1ft 11½in narrow gauge line, was bought by the Southern Railway (SR) in 1923, but closed in 1935.

The LSWR had been a partner with the Midland Railway in the Somerset & Dorset

Railway, and on Grouping the Southern had become a partner of the Midland's successor, the London, Midland & Scottish Railway (LMS).

Due to its geographical location, the Southern was the main provider of packet shipping services across the English Channel, operating from the ports of Dover, Folkestone, Newhaven and Southampton, owning the latter. Its ferry services from Southampton to the Channel Islands of Jersey and Guernsey were operated in collaboration with those of the Great Western Railway from Weymouth.

▼ One of the more powerful LB&SCR locomotives was this '12' class 4-4-2T, which would have been used on expresses. Larger tank locomotives were ideal for shorter distance expresses where their lack of coal and water capacity was less important than the ability to be turned around quickly. (Cody Images)

Did You Know?

Until Herbert Ashcombe Walker took the company in hand, the LSWR had not been the most efficient railway company either. It would send trains from Waterloo to the West Country at ten-minute intervals, but sending the slowest first with a corresponding impact to the schedules of the faster trains following.

The Big Four railway companies each had their own way of coping with the integration of so many smaller companies. For many, it seemed that the Southern tried to pretend that Grouping hadn't happened.

At Victoria, the company inherited a terminus divided into two, one for the London, Brighton & South Coast Railway, and the other for the South East & Chatham Railways (SECR). At first, these were known officially as Victoria (Central Section) for the former LB&SCR lines and Victoria (Eastern Section) for the former SECR lines. It was not until 1924, the year after Grouping, that

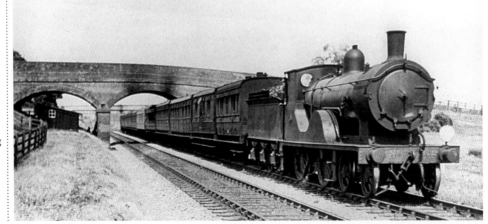

➤ By the early 1930s, many locomotives had strayed away from their original territory, such as this ex-LSWR T-9 heading a Bognor train, and the rake of carriages includes a Pullman car. All of this was very much in line with LB&SCR practice. (HMRS)

the first passageway was opened between the two stations, with a second later in the year and a stationmaster appointed for the entire station. Despite this, separate booking offices remained and it was not until 1938 that a new line and points were installed so that trains from one section could cross into the other.

▲ Despite the impetus for modernisation from electrification, much pre-Grouping rolling stock survived not just the Southern years, but also nationalisation, so this former LB&SCR carriage was still around in 1958. (HMRS)

▲ More distinctive was this former SECR open carriage, almost certainly intended for use on trains with a conductor-guard, possibly with push-pull working. (HMRS)

All this seems like undue haste compared to the other terminus used by the LB&SCR and SECR, London Bridge. It was not until 1928 that a hole was knocked through the wall separating the two stations and a footbridge built to facilitate movement across the station, so passengers coming off the Brighton line could continue their journey to Cannon Street, Charing Cross or Waterloo. The former LSWR under the Southern became the Western Section; the LB&SCR became the Central Section; and

➤ While the Southern Railway was always very reluctant to close lines or stations, this view of Southampton West would today be simply described as 'Southampton'. An ex-LSWR 0-4-2 A12 locomotive has a substantial train, possibly headed for Bournemouth. (HMRS)

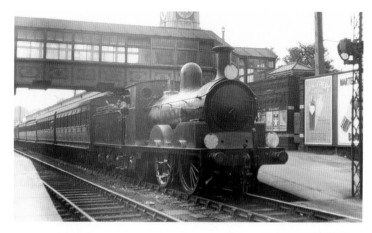

Did You Know?

When a stationmaster was appointed for the whole of Victoria Station, after access was provided between the old LB&SCR, known as the Brighton Side, and the former SECR station, he telegraphed friends saying: 'I have been given twins.'

➤ How many passengers on the lines from Ryde and Newport to Cowes would have guessed that this carriage had started life with the old SECR when they travelled in it in 1964, not many years before the closure of the line by British Railways? (HMRS)

► The LB&SCR had many tank locomotives, including some powerful examples, but this was a 0-6-0 tender locomotive mainly used for goods trains. (HMRS)

the SECR, the Eastern Section. Nevertheless, a fourth section was added, the London Section, for suburban services, many of which ran into more than one section. This still failed to acknowledge inter-section running, such as between Portsmouth and Brighton, or to Portsmouth from Victoria via Arundel and Chichester.

Even as late as 1925, overhead electrification continued on the former

LB&SCR lines, and it was not until 1926 that the Southern announced that it would standardise all electrification on the third rail system.

On the Isle of Wight, the Southern moved quickly to integrate the three small companies on the island, who had sought a mini-grouping of their own but had been denied.

◄ The London & South Western Railway did not have a policy of naming its locomotives, but decided to do so for the publicity benefits. The first class to be named was the 4-6-0 'N15', which became the King Arthur class. This is *Sir Constantine*, preserved in British Railways' livery. (Cody Images)

◀◀ Unnamed but with a tender full of coal and ready to go, is this 'N' class A626, waiting at Nine Elms and perhaps about to take a train to Portsmouth in pre-electrification days. (Cody Images)

◀ Behind the scenes and largely out of sight, this was the reality of the steam railway as rebuilt Battle of Britain-class *65 Squadron* coaled at Nine Elms, the locomotive depot for Waterloo, serving the busy main lines to the West of England, Southampton and Bournemouth. (Cody Images)

The Southern Railway inherited one of the youngest general managers in Sir Herbert Ashcombe Walker, who had been the last general manager of the LSWR. During the First World War he was a member of the Railway Executive, and was effectively its chairman in place of the President of the Board of Trade, for which he received his knighthood.

Voted by the readers of the magazine *Modern Railways* as the outstanding railwayman of all time, Walker was in the LSWR's tradition of recruiting its general managers from outside, in his case from the London & North Western Railway (LNWR) which he had joined at the age of 17. He joined the LSWR in 1912 when he was 43 years old, when it had already started on third rail electrification and on the massive and desperately needed reconstruction of Waterloo.

He completed electrification of the suburban network and extended it to the coast so that by 1939, the third rail covered the Sussex coastline as far east as Hastings, and spread into Hampshire as far as Portsmouth and, well inland, Aldershot and Alton. He extended the docks at Southampton which enabled it to become Britain's premier passenger port at a time when overseas travel meant travel by sea. Others credit him with even interval or 'clockface' scheduling, on which he insisted, but many of the early railways had operated on such a basis, especially on suburban services where high frequency lent itself to even interval operations.

Walker had a strong grasp of financial matters coupled with what can only be described as common sense. Typical of him was the decision not to rebuild the whole of Waterloo because of the 'Windsor' station, which at the time was a new structure and could be incorporated into the reconstruction design without damaging the completeness of the new terminus. Equally, one suspects that his enthusiasm for third rail electrification was based on the economy of a system that did not require the wholesale reconstruction of tunnels and overbridges. Carriages originally built for steam haulage were rebuilt as suburban electric multiple units, again a worthwhile economy, especially as the newer rolling stock was selected which otherwise could have been wasted by premature retirement.

Walker retired in 1937 and became a non-executive director of the Southern until nationalisation. He died in 1949.

The Southern's first chief mechanical engineer was Richard Maunsell, who had also been recruited from outside, joining the SECR from the Great Southern & Western Railway of Ireland. He had also worked in

◀ It needed strong commitment from the very top of a railway company to drive through electrification and Sir Herbert Ashcombe Walker, the first general manager of the Southern Railway, did this and also enlarged and modernised the major port of Southampton. (NRM)

India and for the Lancashire & Yorkshire Railway.

During his time at the Southern, Maunsell was responsible for the highly successful

➤ It was not until Oliver Bulleid joined the company from the LNER that the need for large Pacific steam locomotives was addressed. Bulleid avoided streamlining and instead opted for 'air-smoothed' locomotives, with his Pacifics nicknamed 'spam cans' as a result. (NRM)

Did You Know?

Sir Herbert Walker was known for keeping a tight control on budgets. When in charge of the LSWR, he left the newest part of Waterloo Station untouched during rebuilding. Despite it having a lower roofline than the train shed, he felt that the 'Windsor' platforms did not need modernising.

4-4-0 Schools class, as well as heavy 4-6-0 and 0-6-0 locomotives for goods. His main work, however, was on electrification and during his tenure the Southern limited funds for steam locomotive development because of the capital demands of electrification. A major disappointment for Maunsell was the rejection by the civil engineer of his plans for a four-cylinder 4-6-2 express locomotive and for three-cylinder 2-6-2 locomotives. Nevertheless, in addition to building new rolling stock for the main-line electrification programme, it was also possible to update

◀ Bulleid produced three electric locomotives for the Southern during the Second World War, intended mainly for goods trains. For safety's sake, the third rail in marshalling yards was replaced by overhead wires so that shunters on foot would not be at risk of electrification. (NRM)

the steam-hauled passenger carriages along similar lines.

Maunsell concentrated locomotive work on Ashford and Eastleigh, introducing modern line production methods. He effectively sidelined the old LB&SCR works at Brighton and Lancing, although these were run down rather than closed.

He retired in 1937. Maunsell's successor was Oliver Bulleid, also with considerable experience at home and abroad, and recruited in 1937 from the London & North Eastern Railway (LNER), where he had been assistant to Sir Nigel Gresley, the company's CME.

Bulleid inherited a railway in which the development of larger and more powerful locomotives had been neglected, partly due to the demands of electrification but also because of weight restrictions on many lines. He pressed successfully for the introduction of powerful 4-6-2 locomotives, and overcame severe wartime restrictions on the type and size of locomotives that could be built by claiming that his new designs were for general-purpose duties. He built no less than 140 Pacific locomotives of the Merchant Navy, West Country and Battle of Britain classes, introducing many new features such as completely enclosed chain-driven valve gear and welded fireboxes, and an improved working environment for the enginemen. At the other end of the scale, he produced an austerity 0-6-0 freight locomotive, the 'Q1' class, of outstanding ugliness.

The Bulleid Pacifics incorporated many features that were to be introduced into post-nationalisation designs, including poor forward visibility, and were prone to often catastrophic mechanical failures. His attempt at producing a steam locomotive capable of working at express speeds in either direction, and based on current thinking

Far more successful and enduring was his work on new passenger rolling stock, using a design with widened bodies to provide greater comfort on main-line stock and additional seating on suburban stock in the 4 SUB classes; post-nationalisation these features carried over on to the 2 and 4 EPB and 2 HAP classes.

Post-war, Bulleid worked on a successful design for a prototype 1Co-1Co diesel-electric locomotive, the precursor of 350 locomotives for British Railways, but his anger at the rebuilding of his own Pacific class, despite some of the features being incorporated into the new British Railways standard class, led him to resign in 1949 and join CIE, the Irish transport undertaking, as CME for the railways.

In 1937 Walker's successor as general manager was Gilbert Szlumper, who was unusual in that he was a career LSWR railwayman and the son of Alfred Szlumper,

on electric and diesel designs, resulted in the Leader class of C-C or 0-6-6-0 layout, which failed to pass the prototype stage, not least because of the great discomfort suffered by the fireman.

Did You Know?

When Walker's immediate subordinates debated the colour scheme for the Southern, his solution was to dive into an optician's, buy a length of green spectacle cord, cut it into four, keeping one piece for himself, and insist that this be the future colour reference for passenger steam locomotives and passenger carriages.

the LSWR's chief engineer, who had been behind the work of reconstruction at Waterloo.

Gilbert Szlumper's early career had been in engineering, but in 1913 he became assistant to the new general manager, Herbert Walker, and during the First World War he followed Walker on to the Railway Executive Committee as its secretary. After the war he became the LSWR's docks and marine manager and started the planning for the massive extension of Southampton Docks. He rejoined Walker as assistant general manager of the Southern Railway in 1925.

Szlumper completed most of the Southern's electrification programme with the exception of the direct line to Hastings, for which work was prevented by the outbreak of the Second World War. Once again, Szlumper was required for the wartime railways, being loaned from the Southern to become Director-General of Transportation at the War Office shortly after war broke out. He was retired officially from the Southern in 1942 to become

Director-General at the Ministry of Supply until the war ended.

Szlumper was succeeded by Sir Eustace Missenden, who also came from a railway family, with his father a stationmaster in Kent. He had joined the South Eastern & Chatham Railway in 1899 as a junior clerk, but made rapid progress to become a district traffic superintendent and became a divisional operating superintendent for the Southern in 1923. In the years before the Second World War, Missenden was assistant superintendent of operations in 1930, docks and marine manager at Southampton in 1933, and traffic manager in 1936. He became acting general manager in 1939 when Szlumper was seconded to the War Office, and became general manager in 1942 with Szlumper's transfer to the Ministry of Supply.

In the preparations for nationalisation Missenden became chairman of the Railway Executive Committee, after Sir James Milne of the GWR had rejected the post. Missenden was a Southern man through and through, and, not surprisingly, he found the Railway Executive uncongenial. In addition, he found its relationship with the British Transport Commission, the 'catch-all' body for all nationalised transport industries, difficult, so he retired in 1951.

With Missenden away preparing for nationalisation, John Elliott was appointed acting general manager for the Southern. A former journalist on the *London Evening Standard*, Elliott had joined the Southern in 1925 as public relations assistant to Sir Herbert, but in 1930 he became assistant traffic manager and then proceeded up the company's career ladder to become assistant general manager in 1938. In 1951, as Sir John Elliott, he became chairman of the Railway Executive Committee.

The Southern was at the forefront of all Britain's main-line railways in electrification, maintaining a rolling programme of work until interrupted by the outbreak of the Second World War in 1939.

Both the London & Southern Western and the London Brighton & South Coast Railways had started electrification before the start of the First World War, but using completely different systems. The LSWR had preferred the third rail direct current, or DC, system, which was cheaper to install and required little in the way of major engineering work, although it did require more substations. The LB&SCR had opted for overhead, or 'elevated' in the language of the day, alternating current (AC) electrification. The SECR had still to start electrification, but was planning to use an overhead system, albeit one that was incompatible with that in use by the LB&SCR!

The LB&SCR had been first to introduce electrification, prompted by the need to compete with electric trams, using the South London Line linking its termini at Victoria and London Bridge in 1909. This proved so successful that in 1912 it was followed by the lines to Crystal Palace and Selhurst. The LSWR electrified its line to Wimbledon via East Putney in 1915, and the Kingston and Hounslow loops followed in 1916, including the Shepperton branch and the branch line to Guildford as far as Claygate. The demands of the war put an end to further work.

Although the LSWR must have been tempted to pursue third rail electrification, an independent consultant was commissioned to review the three available methods. While the report was awaited, work proceeded on further electrification with new overhead electrification on the former LB&SCR lines,

▶ The first LSWR suburban electric multiple units were known as the 3 SUB, with three carriages. This train consists of two 3 SUB units at Wimbledon in 1926. Note that even at this early stage before main-line electrification started, both the main line and the local lines have been equipped with the third rail. (HMRS)

A driver's eye view from the cab of a 3 SUB at Queen's Road, between Clapham Junction and Waterloo, in 1923, with the driving cab of another 3 SUB to the left. (HMRS)

Wandsworth Road after the South London line had been converted from overhead, or 'elevated electric'. The line was the first to be electrified by the LB&SCR in response to competition from electric tramways. (HMRS)

with the lines to Coulsdon North and Sutton completed in 1925. In many cases stations were rebuilt and junctions altered, and new stations were also constructed to serve

Did You Know?

An indication of the significance of the Southern's suburban electric system, and the passenger growth generated by this, was shown when the London Passenger Transport Board was formed in 1933 and all suburban receipts, less costs, were to be apportioned between the Big Four railways companies and the LPTB's underground trains. The Southern's share was no less than 25.5 per cent, several times more than any other railway company.

33

the rapidly expanding suburbs. Eastern Section electrification of the old SECR lines also started, even though the decision to standardise on third rail electrification was not reached until 1926. Guildford and Dorking North were reached in 1925.

Electric trains were much faster than steam trains on busy suburban routes with

➤ While main-line trains consisted of new carriages, those for suburban use were often converted from steam-hauled rolling stock, an efficient means of using carriages with life left in them. This 3 SUB consists of ex-LB&SCR carriages. (HMRS)

◀ The 6 PUL electric multiple units maintained the Brighton line tradition of including a Pullman car on express and fast trains instead of a restaurant car, as on such short services only a single sitting was possible at meal times. The Pullman car is the fourth carriage from the front. (HMRS)

▲ After the Eastbourne electrification, 6 PUL units found their way to both Eastbourne and Hastings, often coupled to a 6 PAN as far as Eastbourne. It was to be many years before the direct line to Hastings from London was electrified. (HMRS)

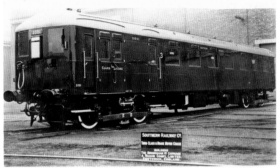

▲ A pre-delivery shot of a motor coach. Brake, second open carriage, for a 6 PUL set for the Brighton electrification. Note the prominent display of third class by the doors, although it was unlikely that first-class passengers would be misled and there was no second class by this time. (HMRS)

◄ The 6 PAN units were easily identifiable with revised window arrangements on the open driving cars, which were still driving brake motor coaches, and, of course, by the substitution of a pantry car for a Pullman. (HMRS)

many stops, which showed the superior acceleration of electric trains. The journey between Waterloo and Guildford via Cobham had taken between seventy-three and seventy-nine minutes by steam train, but fell to fifty-two minutes by electric train. It takes much longer today. Generally, suburban trains ran every thirty minutes off peak and every twenty minutes during the peak period, when trains were often lengthened.

The world's first four-aspect colour-light signalling was introduced between Holborn Viaduct and Elephant & Castle in 1926.

Electricity supply was less advanced than today, especially at industrial power ratings, so a number of schemes were delayed for a month or more because of supply problems. Nevertheless, electrification went ahead, despite the need for often extensive civil engineering works due to the poor state of the old SECR lines, bridges and stations. By 1929, conversion of the overhead to third rail was completed. The following year, with electrification reaching Windsor and Gravesend, suburban electrification was complete.

Before 1930 Walker had already decided to electrify the main lines, telling a meeting of his officers that he had decided to electrify to Brighton. The decision was no doubt helped by the fact that in 1929 the then Chancellor of the Exchequer, Winston Churchill, had abolished Railway Passenger Duty on all fares above 1*d* per mile, on condition that the sums be capitalised and used for the modernisation of the railways. The Southern's capitalised sum was £2 million, while the cost of electrifying the main line to Brighton and West Worthing was estimated at £2.7 million.

On this occasion, electrification was accompanied by the extension of colour-light signalling. The existing steam service was to be replaced by electric trains with frequencies more than doubled, while stopping and semi-fast services would be quicker. The non-stop services, however, would take about the same time due to the lower maximum speeds of the electric trains of the day. On suburban electrification many trains consisted of converted steam-hauled carriages, but for the main-line services new rolling stock was built, usually by independent manufacturers rather than in the Southern's own workshops.

Work started in 1931, and the official inauguration of the through service to Brighton took place at the end of 1932. Rolling stock included the world's first

➤ For local services, especially between Brighton and Eastbourne, 2 NOL electric multiple units were provided, each with a third-class carriage and a composite carriage. (HMRS)

electric all-Pullman train, the 'Brighton Belle', while many others included a Pullman car or additional first-class accommodation. Off peak there were six trains an hour, with four running to and from Victoria, and the others running to and from London Bridge. As with the suburban electrification, trains were arranged as self-propelled electric multiple units, but the fast trains were usually of six cars rather than the three cars of the suburban stock. The 'Brighton Belle', when it was introduced in 1934, had three five-car units designated as 5 BEL, one of which was held as a spare. Stopping and semi-fast services on the Brighton line

◀ A 6 PAN heads towards London in 1935. As no further 6 PUL units were built, both the Brighton and Eastbourne trains often consisted of a 6 PAN and a 6 PUL, offering a wider variety of accommodation and a choice in catering. (HMRS)

▶ A 4 COR speeds from Waterloo to Woking on the 'Portsmouth Direct'. The distinguishing feature was the provision of corridor connections through the driving cabs and the use of four car units, allowing greater flexibility in the total accommodation provided. This train is bound for Portsmouth Harbour as it has an '8' headcode, with '7' used on trains terminating at Portsmouth & Southsea. (HMRS)

40

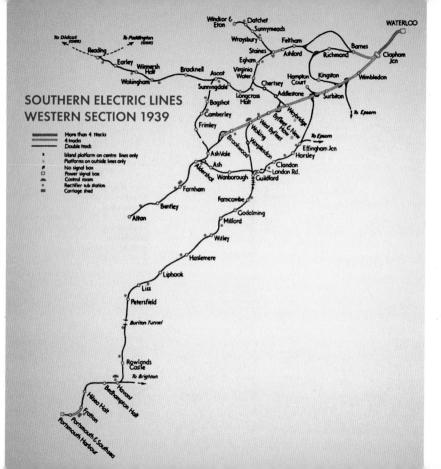

SOUTHERN ELECTRIC LINES
WESTERN SECTION 1939

More than 4 tracks
4 tracks
Double track
Island platform on centre lines only
Platforms on outside lines only
No signal box
Power signal box
Control room
Rectifier sub station
Carriage shed

◄◄ The other new electric multiple unit for the Portsmouth electrification was the 2 BIL, with both carriages having a corridor and toilets. These units worked the Portsmouth and Alton stopping services, the Reading and Ascot, and Portsmouth–Brighton trains. (NRM)

◄ The Southern perpetuated the old pre-Grouping divisions with separate sections. This is the Western Section electrification, or the old LSWR! (Southern Railway)

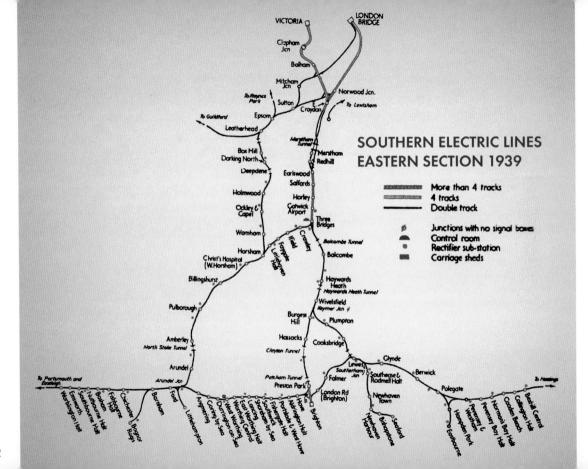

SOUTHERN ELECTRIC LINES
EASTERN SECTION 1939

Legend:
- More than 4 tracks
- 4 tracks
- Double track

- ∅ Junctions with no signal boxes
- ● Control room
- ● Rectifier sub-station
- ▬ Carriage sheds

Stations and features (as labelled):

VICTORIA · LONDON BRIDGE · Clapham Jcn · Balham · Mitcham Jcn · Norwood Jcn. · Sutton · Croydon · To Raynes Park · To Guildford · Epsom · To Lewisham · Leatherhead · Merstham Tunnel · Merstham · Box Hill · Redhill · Dorking North · Earlswood · Deepdene · Salfords · Holmwood · Horley · Ockley & Capel · Gatwick Airport · Three Bridges · Warnham · Crawley · Ifield · Balcombe Tunnel · Horsham · Faygate · Littlehaven Halt · Balcombe · Christ's Hospital (W.Horsham) · Billingshurst · Haywards Heath · Haywards Heath Tunnel · Pulborough · Wivelsfield · Keymer Jcn · Burgess Hill · Plumpton · Amberley · North Stoke Tunnel · Hassocks · Cooksbridge · Clayton Tunnel · Glynde · Arundel · Lewes · Southerham Jcn · Berwick · To Portsmouth and Eastleigh · Arundel Jcn · Folmer · Southease & Rodmell Halt · Polegate · To Hastings · Patcham Tunnel · Preston Park · Hove · Aldrington Halt · Portslade & West Hove · London Rd (Brighton) · Newhaven Town · Bexhill Central · Emsworth · Warblington Halt · Southbourne · Bosham · Fishbourne Halt · Fratton · Chichester · Bognor Regis · Barnham · Ford · Littlehampton · Angmering · Goring-by-Sea · Worthing Central · West Worthing · Durrington-on-Sea · East Worthing Halt · Lancing · Shoreham Halt · Southwick · Fishersgate Halt · Portslade · Brighton · Kingston Halt · Bishopstone · Newhaven Harbour · Seaford · To Eastbourne · Hampden Park · Pevensey & Westham · Pevensey Bay Halt · Normans Bay Halt · Cooden Beach · Collington Halt

42

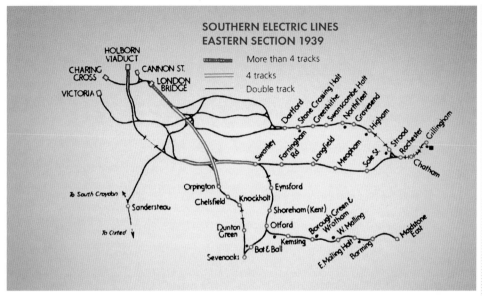

SOUTHERN ELECTRIC LINES
EASTERN SECTION 1939

········· More than 4 tracks
━━━━━ 4 tracks
═══ Double track

HOLBORN VIADUCT
CHARING CROSS
CANNON ST.
LONDON BRIDGE
VICTORIA

Dartford
Stone Crossing Halt
Greenhithe
Swanscombe Halt
Northfleet
Gravesend
Higham
Strood
Rochester
Gillingham
Chatham
Swanley
Farningham Rd
Longfield
Meopham
Sole St.

To South Croydon
Sanderstead
To Oxted

Orpington
Chelsfield
Knockholt
Eynsford
Shoreham (Kent)
Otford
Dunton Green
Kemsing
Bat & Ball
Sevenoaks
Borough Green & Wrotham
W. Malling
E. Malling Halt
Barming
Maidstone East

◀◀ The former 'Brighton', or LB&SCR electrification, was known as the Central Section, but of course went much further than the LB&SCR had ever done and was the first main-line electrification, reaching the coast at the end of 1932. (Southern Railway)

◀ The SECR was too impoverished to begin electrification before Grouping, but the Southern pressed ahead and the third rail reached Gillingham and Maidstone before the outbreak of war brought work to a stop. (Southern Railway)

were operated by four-car units designated 4 LAV, as one of the carriages had a lavatory at each end. Two-car sets, designated 2 NOL, were ordered for local services between Brighton and Eastbourne when electrification was extended to Eastbourne and on to Hastings in 1935.

Other electrification followed, with Portsmouth Harbour being reached from Waterloo via Guildford in 1937, when

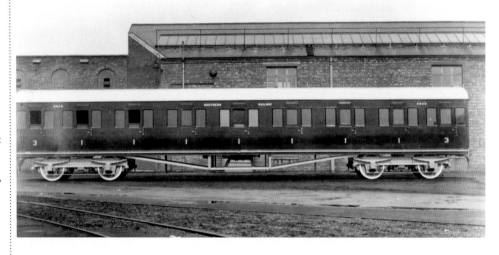

➤ The final pre-war, and indeed pre-nationalisation, electrification was on the Eastern Section, the former SECR lines, and this picture shows how the Southern signed its passenger rolling stock. (HMRS)

➤➤ A wartime expedient was to convert the 3 SUB units to 4 SUB by simply inserting an additional trailer carriage, something not so easily achieved with modern rolling stock. (HMRS)

the line to Aldershot and Alton was also electrified. A year later, the line from Victoria to Portsmouth via Arundel and Chichester was electrified, along with the lines to Bognor and Littlehampton, and Brighton–Portsmouth services. The first Portsmouth electrification saw fast trains run between the Hampshire town and Waterloo in just ninety-five minutes instead of the two hours taken by steam trains due to the heavy gradients on the line; the service also increased from four fast trains

➤ Most purpose-built 4
SUBs consisted of a mix of
open and compartment
coaches without corridors.
The overall effect was
pleasing and an eight-car
train could seat more than
800 passengers. (NRM)

a day to up to four an hour on a summer Saturday. Four-car units were used for the fast and semi-fast trains, and for the first time there were corridor connections through the driving cabs. Trains normally ran as eight or twelve cars.

Before the outbreak of the Second World War, the Southern extended its electrification to Reading in the west and to Gillingham and Maidstone in the east. A new line was built to cater for the expansion of London's suburbs, running off

the line from Waterloo to Dorking North and reaching Tolworth in May 1938, and Chessington South a year later. It was, of course, electrified throughout.

The electrification into Kent saw a new class of multiple units introduced, the 2 HAL, with a powered or motor coach that had a guard's compartment and a composite trailer, once again with a lavatory and side corridor.

Wartime brought demands for additional rolling stock for the suburban services,

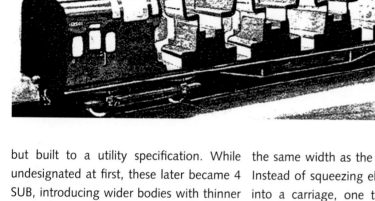

The Bulleid style was retained for the two 4 DD double-deck prototypes, which normally operated as a single train on services to and from Charing Cross. As the drawing shows, access was not easy as passengers reached the upper compartments by moving through the lower compartments. (NRM)

but built to a utility specification. While undesignated at first, these later became 4 SUB, introducing wider bodies with thinner carriage sides. Not only could passengers be seated six-abreast in carriages without a gangway, but one carriage had eleven compartments squeezed in to a length usually limited to ten compartments. These carriages had standard driving cab ends, but post-war, further units were built with ends the same width as the rest of the carriage. Instead of squeezing eleven compartments into a carriage, one trailer had just nine compartments in case first class returned to inner suburban services – it didn't.

As we will see in the next chapter, post-war the Southern produced both electric engines and diesel-electric locomotives, although the latter did not appear until after nationalisation.

The body style and accommodation was retained for the 4 EPB units introduced after nationalisation, with electro-pneumatic braking. The pleasing appearance was improved by roller blinds for the route number display. (HMRS)

49

While the priority for the Southern Railway was electrification, steam could not be ignored. Not only did the company inherit a massive stock of steam locomotives, it was clear that many lines, especially in north Devon and north Cornwall where the company had extensive track mileage, and in the south of Devon and Dorset where many smaller resorts were served, could not justify the high investment of electrification. As the company neared the end of its days, diesel working for these lines was considered, but in the 1920s and 1930s, steam was the obvious choice for longer-distance express passenger work.

While the Great Western had consciously decided against adopting the 4-6-2 Pacific steam locomotive and had converted its only example to a 4-6-0 configuration, the Southern wanted Pacifics, but couldn't afford them while the push to electrify went ahead. Electrification also released many steam locomotives which could be cascaded on to other services. For example, ex-LSWR '02' class 0-4-4 tank engines were sent to the Isle of Wight, accompanied by a smaller number of ex-LB&SCR 'Terrier' 0-6-0 tank engines for lines which could not take the heavier '02'. The Isle of Wight steam locomotives were amongst the few small tank engines to be named, after the towns and villages on the island. Despite this, the company did produce some fine 4-4-0 and 4-6-0 steam locomotives for its express services.

Maunsell's time at the SECR was limited by the First World War, which prevented him acquiring the new and more powerful locomotives that the merged operation needed now that its damaging rivalries had been overcome. It was not until 1917

The scene at the end of the branch line to Seaton in south Devon, with a tank engine sandwiched between two passenger carriages and a horsebox! Today, the line is closed to trains but survives with a tramway running between Seaton and Seaton Junction on the line between Basingstoke and Exeter. (HMRS)

that the first of his new class of mixed traffic locomotives, the 'N' class 2-6-0, appeared, and by the time of Grouping just eleven more were completed. Production was continued by the Southern, with later versions having three cylinders and known as the 'N1'. Fitted with 6ft wheels instead of the original 5ft 6in wheels, the design

➤ Shortly before nationalisation, a 'K10' locomotive waits at Eastleigh with a train to Portsmouth via Fareham and Portchester. Before the direct line between London Waterloo and Portsmouth opened, this would have been the LSWR main line from London to Portsmouth. (HMRS)

formed the basis of the Southern's 2-6-4T 'K' class, more usually known as the River class until later rebuilt as tender locomotives and redesignated as the 'U' class.

More powerful express locomotives were needed for the services to the Channel ports and for those out of Waterloo, on which the Southern's longer distance

services were concentrated. Maunsell improved Harry Wainwright's 'L' class, with higher boiler pressure, as the 'L1', but the increasing number of corridor carriages meant heavier trains and a more powerful design was needed. Robert W. Urie's 'N15' class 4-6-0 locomotives were also updated with improved valve gear and blast arrangements, with additional locomotives built as the King Arthur class – the first Southern class to have named locomotives in a bid to improve publicity.

The first of the Southern's completely new locomotive classes was a 4-6-0, the Lord Nelson class, named after famous admirals. When introduced in 1926, the Lord Nelsons were the most powerful locomotives in the country and provided the basis for the Royal Scot class of the LMS. Wheel size was 6ft 7in, and the four-cylinder locomotives could handle a 500-ton express. Trials were conducted with slightly smaller wheels to see if performance could be improved on the more steeply graded lines, but no significant improvement was experienced. Experiments with special blast pipes and a double chimney showed that while performance was boosted, it was at the cost of higher coal consumption.

The Southern inherited many difficult main lines with tight curvatures on bends and loading gauge restrictions, reflecting

Did You Know?

One of the first Southern locomotives to be named was the King Arthur-class *Joyous Gard*, using names from the legend of King Arthur. Managers were concerned about opposition from the guards and the National Union of Railwaymen. The only objection came when an official of the drivers' and firemen's union, ASLEF, telephoned the company secretary and demanded: 'This *Joyous Gard*, what about the bleeding driver, then?'

◄ Coaling the hard way. Mechanised coaling was spreading across Britain's railways but the tight confines of the Guildford shed meant that there was no real incentive for heavy investment in facilities for steam locomotives at this busy Surrey town. (HMRS)

the poverty of the companies that had previously served the newly named Eastern Section. This led to the Schools class, named after famous public schools, which was a 4-4-0 locomotive using a modified King Arthur-class boiler. The first example appeared in 1930 and was the most powerful 4-4-0 on Britain's railways,

PASSENGERS
MUST CROSS LINE
BY THE BRIDGE

56

◄ Brading, on the busy Isle of Wight line from Ryde to Sandown, Shanklin and Ventnor. Passengers could change here for the branch line to Bembridge, which survived until well after nationalisation, despite the railway journey being less direct than that by road. (HMRS)

➤ An '02' 0-4-4T tank locomotive waits at Ventnor on the Isle of Wight, the end of the busiest of the island lines and where more powerful locomotives were needed, but could not be accommodated because of the tight clearances. (HMRS)

capable of speeds of up to 80mph and working a train of 400 tons.

Less successful was Maunsell's 'Z' class 0-8-0T shunter, which first appeared in 1929, of which just eight were built. The need for such a powerful shunter was limited, and by this time Maunsell was introducing his first diesel-electric shunters, which proved to be far more economical.

Another '02' on the Isle of Wight, seen at Ryde St John's Station which handled trains to both Ventnor and to Newport and Cowes. (HMRS)

His last design was the 'Q' class, not to be confused with the 'Q1' – although both were 0-6-0 tender locomotives – which was actually seen into service by Bulleid. The River-class locomotives had to be rebuilt as tender locomotives after their instability contributed to a serious accident at Sevenoaks.

An 'H15' express locomotive takes an up West of England express towards Waterloo in 1945; the multiple tracks without any sign of a third rail suggest that its location is between Basingstoke and Woking. (HMRS)

When Bulleid arrived from the LNER in 1937, he was determined to ensure that the Southern received the Pacific locomotives that it needed for its heavier and longer-distance expresses. War was approaching and the government was insisting that only mixed traffic locomotives of a standard design could be built. In fact,

➤ The most famous Southern express was the 'Golden Arrow', an all-Pullman train that ran from Victoria to Dover with its own connecting ferry, the *Canterbury*. This is a West Country-class locomotive, *Crewkerne*, taking the train from Victoria. (Cody Images)

◄ The other famous Southern named express was the 'Bournemouth Belle', which ran from Waterloo to Southampton and Bournemouth Central and the now closed Bournemouth West. Here it is in the hands of Merchant Navy-class *French Line CGT*. (Cody Images)

the mainly passenger Southern suddenly found itself short of freight locomotives, and Bulleid introduced his 0-6-0 'Q1' class locomotives which were severely utilitarian in appearance; forty-four were built.

Meanwhile, Bulleid also introduced the Southern's first Pacific locomotives, bypassing official restrictions by using wheels of 6ft 2in diameter, allowing him to claim that the first of these, the Merchant

➤ Heading in the opposite direction with a continental express is LN 4-6-0 *Sir Walter Raleigh* at Knockholt in 1929. (HMRS)

➤➤ King Arthur-class 'N15' *Sir Pelleas* takes an up, or London-bound, express through Headcorn shortly after nationalisation. The carriages are the main-line version of Bulleid's 'wide-bodied' rolling stock. (HMRS)

Navy class, was in fact a mixed traffic locomotive. Early publicity photographs of these locomotives working showed them handling goods trains. They first appeared in 1941 and instead of streamlining, the locomotives were air-smoothed, with an external casing that gave a 'squared-off' appearance that led to the nickname, for

both these and the two lighter-weight classes that followed, 'spam cans'.

The driving mechanism was also unconventional, with a chain drive running through an oil bath, and three cylinders, as well as the highest boiler pressure of any production steam locomotive. The Bulleid Pacifics provided greater driving comfort and a massive improvement in power for the Southern, but they needed considerable attention. Even though the Merchant Navy-class locomotives were designed with the many weight restrictions on the Southern in mind, there was also a need for something lighter still, so the West Country and Battle of Britain classes were conceived to meet this need, while retaining the design features and overall appearance of the larger Merchant Navy class. While the Merchant Navy class had most of the locomotives named after famous shipping lines, the first was called *Channel Packet*

as the Southern was the main operator of cross-Channel ferries. Ironically, they were too heavy to use the lines within Southampton Docks, so boat trains had to be worked by the lighter West Country and Battle of Britain classes.

Finally, Bulleid designed a new class of steam locomotive that was intended to offer the flexibility of a diesel or an electric engine, with a driving cab at each end and designated as 0-6-6-0T, or perhaps a Co-Co in diesel and electric designation. The first appeared shortly after nationalisation, but the location of the fireman, in the middle of the locomotive between the tender and boiler, was so uncomfortable due to the heat and lack of ventilation that only the first prototype was completed and operated for a short period and several more on order were cancelled.

In common with the other railways, the Southern also had a number of US-built

◀ An 'N15' heads an inter-regional train from Birmingham to Brighton through Clapham Junction in 1949, shortly after nationalisation. The train would have come from the West London Line. (HMRS)

▶ The Lord Nelson-class 4-6-0 steam locomotives influenced the design of the LMS Royal Scot class. This is *Lord Anson* imbibing water and looking none too well cared for shortly after nationalisation. (HMRS)

▶▶ The Merchant Navy class was, paradoxically, too heavy to enter Southampton Docks, and with many stretches of line elsewhere also having weight restrictions, Bulleid built a lighter version, the West Country class. This is *Torrington*, with the 'Thanet Belle' Pullman shortly after nationalisation. (HMRS)

tank engines, many of which survived to the end of steam. The greatest survivors were the '02' class 0-4-4Ts on the Isle of Wight; these Victorian locomotives also lasted to the end of steam.

Post-nationalisation, many of the Bulleid Pacifics were rebuilt and, except for the wheels, had a passing similarity in appearance to the Britannia class of British Railways.

The Southern also built a small number of 0-6-0 shunting engines. After the war, Bulleid designed three 'CC' class electric engines for freight trains, which, in addition to the usual third rail conductor shoe, had a simple overhead pick-up, because for safety reasons the goods sidings were fitted with overhead wiring rather than third rail. Two of these engines were delivered before nationalisation. Two diesel-electric locomotives were delivered after nationalisation, and although the motors and subframe were similar to the electric engines, the appearance was slightly less austere. These were transferred to the London Midland Region of British Railways and ran very successfully, providing a basis for the 4X series of diesel electrics. On the Southern, these would have been used for passenger trains on those lines which could not justify electrification, such as those to the West Country.

The Southern Railway was the main operator of ferries across the English Channel to France and Belgium, and shared the Channel Islands traffic with the Great Western. It was also the main operator to the Isle of Wight.

The company inherited the former SECR services from Dover and Folkestone to France and Belgium, and the former LB&SCR service from Newhaven to Dieppe. The old LSWR services to France and the Channel Islands from Southampton

◄ The Southern's shipping services included the short crossing from Portsmouth Harbour to Ryde on the Isle of Wight. The company replaced the ships it had inherited and named them after places on both sides of the Solent. (NRM)

also passed to the Southern. The Channel Island services were coordinated with those of the GWR from Weymouth, a move that had preceded Grouping and was designed in part to stop dangerous racing between LSWR and GWR masters. The LSWR and LB&SCR had operated ferry services from Portsmouth Harbour to Ryde, for foot passengers. It was not until 1928 that a vehicle ferry was introduced between Portsmouth and Fishbourne. A third ferry service was operated for vehicles and passengers between Lymington and Yarmouth, which had been an entirely LSWR affair.

There was another service to the Isle of Wight, from Southampton to Cowes, operated by the Southampton, Isle of Wight & South Coast Royal Mail Steam Packet Company, usually known as Red Funnel, and this appeared in the company's timetables. However, the railway termini at Southampton and Cowes were some distance from the ferry terminal, even though at the time the Southern had a terminus in the docks, as well as the busy Southampton West (now known as Southampton Central) on the main line from Waterloo to Bournemouth and Weymouth.

These routes served different markets, with the cross-Channel services from Dover and Folkestone being much shorter than those from Dieppe, which in turn were much shorter than those from Southampton. While the Southern was slow to ensure that Victoria became a unified terminus, as early as autumn 1923 all of the Dover, Folkestone and Newhaven boat trains were concentrated on Victoria. The SECR had built a new terminus at Dover Marine which considerably eased the transfer between train and ship, but with cross-Channel traffic much less intense than after the Second World War, the platform

◀ On arrival at Ryde, passengers from Portsmouth could board a train for the east of the island or for Newport and Cowes, while those going into the town itself could catch a bus, walk down the long pier or take the petrol-engined tramway, seen here in the background. (HMRS)

at Folkestone was not lengthened from an inadequate 308ft to 700ft until 1938.

Despite the Great Depression of the late 1920s, aggravated in the UK by the General Strike and Miners' Strike of 1926, the Southern started to enhance its cross-Channel services. Even at this early stage, one pressing reason for doing so was the

growing competition from air transport, especially for premium traffic.

In 1924 new ships were introduced at Southampton: the *Dinard* and the *St Briac*. The following year two new ships were introduced on the services between Dover and Calais, and between Folkestone and Boulogne: the *Isle of Thanet* and the *Maid of Kent*, both at around 2,700 tons. The Newhaven–Dieppe service also received new ships, the *Worthing*, 2,294 tons, in 1928, and the *Brighton*, which was slightly larger, in 1933.

In 1929 the Southern introduced the most luxurious through service between London and Paris with the advent of the 'Golden Arrow', an all-Pullman train with a French counterpart, the 'Flèche d'Or', linked by the all-first-class Channel packet *Canterbury*, at 2,910 tons. This was an extravagant gesture as the ship made just one return crossing daily, compared to four for modern ships. Unconcerned, the Southern ordered an even larger ship for the service, the *Invicta*, at 4,178 tons. She was intended to carry first- and third-class passengers, but on delivery in 1939 she was immediately taken up for war service.

These ships were conventional, with no drive-on/drive-off facility as would be expected today. In 1931 a purpose-built car ferry, the *Autocarrier*, was introduced to the Dover–Calais service but vehicles were still craned on and off. It was not until the Southern decided to introduce train ferries to the cross-Channel services that motorists were at last able to drive their cars on and off the ships, with a special 'garage' deck for twenty-five cars. Three ships were ordered – the *Twickenham Ferry*, the *Hampton Ferry* and the *Shepperton Ferry* – each with two railway lines running the full length of the train deck and a siding branching out on each side, providing accommodation for

◀ The 'Night Ferry', with its wagons-lits built to suit the much more confined British loading gauge, provided a through service without changing between London and Paris. (NRM)

➤ Merchant Navy-class *Elder Dempster Lines* gets ready to handle the 'Night Ferry' at Stewart's Lane depot. (HMRS)

twelve sleeping cars. These ships entered service in October 1936, operating the 'Night Ferry' through sleeping car service between London and Paris, of which more is said in the next chapter. Many cross-Channel services were operated jointly with the French railway company, the SNCF, so the *Twickenham Ferry* was transferred to the French flag before the service started to assuage French pride and intransigence!

A much less prestigious service was that between Portsmouth Harbour, where the special station had just a short walk between train and ferry, and Ryde on the Isle of Wight. This was by far the most important service between the mainland and the island. The service had previously been operated jointly by the LB&SCR and the LSWR, and the Southern acted quickly to repaint the white funnels with Southern buff with a black topping. While the newest ship dated from 1911, the oldest had been completed in 1889, so the Southern introduced a steady stream of new ships, all coal-fired paddle steamers. Instead of naming them after duchesses, the company introduced a policy of naming them after places on either side of the Solent: first came *Shanklin* in 1924; then *Merstone* and *Portsdown* in 1928; followed by the *Southsea* and *Whippingham* in 1930; *Sandown* in 1934; and *Ryde* in 1939.

The Lymington–Yarmouth service was also modernised, with two ships, *Lymington*, built in 1893, and *Solent II*, dating from 1902, being joined by the *Freshwater* in 1927. Cars were carried on this service, but they were towed in barges behind the ferries.

The main service for motor vehicles to and from the Isle of Wight was between Southampton and Cowes, and this market was growing, not just because car ownership was increasing, but also because bus and coach services were flourishing. Tidal problems and the shallow waters offshore meant that Ryde was not suitable for a car ferry, but eventually the Southern found a suitable spot in Wootton Creek at Fishbourne, while an appropriate slipway was found in Portsmouth at Broad Street near Old Portsmouth. The Southern's service was inaugurated in 1928 with two double-end drive-on/drive-off ferries, the

Fishbourne and *Wootton*, and proved so successful that a third ship, *Hilsea*, was introduced in 1930. These ships had limited passenger accommodation for the occupants of the cars, but they meant that the barges at Lymington were seen as no longer satisfactory, and a purpose-built ferry, the *Lymington*, was introduced in 1938, able to carry passengers off the trains on the branch line as well as those who came in the cars.

The great port of Southampton owed much of its success to the LSWR, which encouraged its development and promoted it as a calling point for liners that would otherwise have used London as their British port. This saved the best part of a day on the voyage, and in the late nineteenth century it meant that the often hazardous voyage around the North Foreland was avoided. This put the port in competition with the GWR at Plymouth, but passengers could land direct at Southampton, and as the port was more convenient for London than Liverpool, liners going to Liverpool began to switch to the south coast port.

All of this was encouraged by the Southern as it developed the port even further. An Ocean Terminal with a railway

THE NEW TRAIN FERRY BOATS

| SLEEPING CARS EVERY NIGHT between LONDON (VICTORIA) and PARIS | VIA DOVER-DUNKERQUE | FAST THROUGH SERVICES EVERY DAY for GOODS, CARS & PERISHABLE TRAFFIC |

Full details of Services, Fares, Rates, etc., from
SOUTHERN RAILWAY CONTINENTAL DEPARTMENT, VICTORIA STATION, S.W.I.

◄ The Southern proudly advertised the new train ferries, which were described in typical railway fashion as 'boats'. Of the three built, one had to be transferred to the French flag to assuage national pride. (NRM/Science & Society Picture Library)

connection was built in the older part of the docks, while further upstream the new West Docks, again with a railway connection, were built on reclaimed land. The port became the UK landfall for companies such as Cunard, United States Lines, French Lines, the Peninsular & Oriental (P&O) and Union Castle.

Even in Southern Railway days, the company was viewed mainly as a commuter railway, and with the exception of its services to the West Country, there were no long-distance expresses to compare with those chasing up and down the East and West Coast main lines. Yet the first named express had come not from the grand companies with their long-distance travellers, but from the poverty-stricken South Eastern Railway with its 'Granville Special Express' linking London and Ramsgate in 1876.

The LSWR had no history of named trains, and even the LB&SCR only had the 'Southern Belle', an all-Pullman express linking Brighton and London Victoria, which, after electrification, was replaced by the 'Brighton Belle'.

The main Southern expresses included the following:

The 'Atlantic Coast Express', whose name was picked from a winning entry in a competition in the *Southern Railway Magazine*. The train first appeared in July 1926, leaving Waterloo at 11 a.m. daily for Ilfracombe and Plymouth, dividing at Exeter, but was also applied to the following 11.10 a.m. for Bude and Padstow. Portions were also dropped for other destinations, such as Sidmouth and Exmouth. Frequently, a single through carriage would be attached to a local stopping train for the final few miles of the journey. New rolling stock was not provided until 1928 and because of its many portions, the train required an unusually high number of brake composite carriages.

The 'Bournemouth Belle' was introduced for the summer 1931 timetable and operated from Waterloo to Southampton and Bournemouth, where it divided and

◀◀ An aerial view of the western extremity of the Southern Railway, showing Padstow, then a railway terminus, with one of the tavern cars built for the 'Atlantic Coast Express' prominent in the foreground. This is a post-nationalisation shot as the carriages are in carmine and cream livery. (HMRS)

◀ In an attempt to boost the popularity of the 'Atlantic Coast Express', the catering carriages were finished to resemble a West Country inn, with a tavern car as shown here. It was not especially popular, possibly because the interior was dark and gloomy, with no opportunity to view the passing countryside. (HMRS)

sent five carriages onwards to Poole, Wareham, Dorchester and Weymouth, while the rest of the train continued to Bournemouth West. The train ran daily in the summer months, but only on Sundays in winter. It took eighty-nine minutes to cover the 80 miles to Southampton West (now known as Southampton Central),

Did You Know?

The 'Night Ferry' consisted of wagons-lits (sleeping cars), providing through journeys between London and Paris without the need to change between ship and train. While great care was taken to shunt the carriages between shore and ship quietly and smoothly, sleep was interrupted as the carriages were chained to the deck of the ship. In contrast to today, when passengers are not allowed on to the vehicle decks of car ferries while crossing the Channel, the passengers aboard the sleeping cars were locked in before the ship set sail.

and 129 minutes to do the 108 miles to Bournemouth Central. As was usual, a Pullman supplement was payable, varying on class and distance, which ranged from 1s 6d for third class between London and Southampton, and 4s for first class between London and Weymouth. There were ten carriages, with the three first-class carriages all given girls' names.

The **'Brighton Belle'** replaced the 'Southern Belle' and was the world's first all-Pullman electric multiple unit train when it appeared in 1934. Unusually for a named train, it ran several times each day, using two 6 PUL units, while other trains with a single Pullman car in each of their 5 BEL units provided additional departures so that between them an hourly service was provided in each direction. The Southern could therefore claim that between Victoria and Brighton the services were 'every hour, on the hour and within the hour'.

◄ Another post-nationalisation view of Bulleid's passenger rolling stock. This might look like a composite brake, but in fact the two nearest compartments were third class, as was the four-bay open section, allowing for individual passenger preferences. (HMRS)

The **'Golden Arrow'** was by far the most famous and prestigious of all the Southern's named trains. It replaced an unnamed Pullman train first introduced in 1926, and was named in 1929 to coincide with the introduction of the all-first-class ferry

The 'Devon Belle' Pullman in the hands of West Country-class *Exeter*, appropriately at Exeter St David's, a station shared by the Southern and the GWR, and later by the Southern and Western Regions of British Railways. This meant there could be trains for London facing in opposite directions. (HMRS)

Canterbury between Dover and Calais. The French counterpart was the *Flèche d'Or*. The train left Victoria at 11.10 a.m. daily and arrived at Dover Marine at 12.35, with a 12.55 sailing and eventual arrival at Paris Nord at 5.35 p.m. In the opposite direction, the train left Paris at noon, reached Calais at 3.10 p.m. and the train left Dover at 4.57 p.m. and arrived at Victoria at 6.35 a.m. Luggage could be booked through with collection and delivery for a small supplement, and London-bound passengers were promised delivery of their luggage that evening.

◄ The 'Brighton Belle' arriving in Brighton in 1933, with a 4 LAV for stopping or semi-fast services in the background. (HMRS)

First-class and composite Pullman carriages were all given girls' names, while third-class Pullmans were simply numbered. This is *Vera* at Victoria Station, an ex-'Brighton Belle' trailer carriage. Today she can be found at the UK end of the 'Orient Express', running from London to Dover. (Phil Scott)

➤➤ The West Country-class locomotive *Templecombe*, rebuilt as an attractive locomotive that was more reliable than her original design. (HMRS)

The **'Night Ferry'** was by contrast the least well known of all the Southern expresses, despite being the most ambitious. Train ferries were not new, with the earliest in the UK dating from 1849, and during the First World War the British Army had a train ferry

based at Richborough in Kent. Interest in an Anglo-French train ferry was aroused in 1930 by French plans for a freight ferry. There were delays while suitable ports

▶ The most famous Southern express was, of course, the 'Golden Arrow' Pullman that handled the cream of the London–Paris boat train traffic and had a French partner in the *Flèche D'Or*, as well as its own all-first-class steamer, *Canterbury*. (NRM/Science & Society Picture Library)

▶▶ All of the railway companies advertised holiday destinations, of which one was Guernsey. The Southern and the GWR continued the pre-Grouping arrangement whereby they operated their services jointly. (NRM/Science & Society Picture Library)

ENSURE A
GOOD
MORNING
travel by
SOUTHERN
ELECTRIC
SPEED COMFORT FREQUENCY

were chosen and then modified and three ferries were constructed, as mentioned in the previous chapter. Wagons-lits were built to the tighter British loading gauge, and

GO BY RAIL WITH A
CHEAP
"MONTHLY RETURN"

That's the Ticket!

Cheap "Monthly Return" Tickets are issued all the year round between most stations and are available by any train any day.

Full particulars from any Railway Station Office or Agency

G.W.R   LMS   L·N·E·R   S.R

◄◄ Having invested heavily in electrification, the Southern did its best to boost traffic, emphasising the speed, comfort and increased frequency of their new services. (NRM/Science & Society Picture Library)

◄ A joint advertising campaign for fares that could be as low as a penny a mile, as the companies struggled to encourage travel during the bleak years of the 1930s. (Railway Companies Association)

one is on display at the National Railway Museum in York, which also has an LNER/SNCF train ferry goods van. One reason for the project being pushed forward at a difficult time for the economy was that the railways were already suffering from competition for premium passenger traffic, and maintained that the 'Night Ferry' was

◀ Another Merchant Navy-class Pacific, *Bibby Line*, takes the down 'Bournemouth Belle' Pullman through Eastleigh. (HMRS)

◀ A composite restaurant car for the 'Atlantic Coast Express' in BR days, although even the steam-hauled stock soon reverted to Southern green, while the electric multiple units remained green until the launch of British Rail, when suburban units became blue and the rest became blue and pale grey. (HMRS)

the only sure way of getting to an early morning meeting in Paris or London!

The service started on 5 October 1936 but was an anti-climax, for on that first night passengers had to leave their sleeping berths and go to cabins aboard the ship. The 'real' start was on 14 October from London and 15 October from Paris. Trains left Victoria at 10 p.m. each evening with an arrival at Paris Nord at 8.55 a.m. In the opposite direction, the train left Paris at 9.50 p.m. to reach Victoria at 8.30 a.m.

The service was suspended a week before the outbreak of the Second World War and only restarted in mid-December 1947, a fortnight before nationalisation, due to industrial disputes in France.

There were many other named trains, but one that was completely unofficial was the **'Flying Boat Train'**. This followed the inauguration of the Empire Air Mail Scheme in 1937. The service was provided by the famous Short Empire 'C' class flying boats of Imperial Airways. Flights left Hythe, near Southampton, on Tuesdays and Thursdays, and on each day a flight would leave for South Africa and another would depart to India and Australia. As the aircraft could only carry twenty-four passengers each, a full train was not required, but one or two Pullman carriages and a brake van for luggage, with roof boards proclaiming 'Imperial Airways Empire Services', were added to a Bournemouth express. The carriages and brake van were detached at Southampton West and shunted into the docks, where passengers alighted and were taken by launch to Hythe.

The Southern was one of the most air-minded of the Big Four railway companies. It was the first to build railway stations at airports, and even sought and identified a site for London's new post-war airport, although the authorities much preferred the old Fairey base near Hounslow that eventually became Heathrow.

Despite the heavy investment in shipping and ports, the railways were amongst the pioneers of domestic air services in the British Isles, with their involvement starting in 1933. Initially, the more ambitious companies acted independently, but a combined operation – Railway Air Services (RAS) – was formed in 1934, involving the Southern as well as the GWR and the LMS. The airlines operating to the Isle of Wight and the Channel Islands collaborated with RAS, as did airlines operating within Scotland. The LMS was not involved when, in 1938, a new airline was formed by the Southern and the GWR: Great Western and Southern Air Services (GWSAS).

RAS and then GWSAS had the support of Imperial Airways, which initially provided pilots and did not operate domestic air services on its own account. The Southern and the GWR then each acquired a 16.5 per cent investment in Channel Islands Airways.

Amongst the services operated was one from Cowes on the Isle of Wight to Southampton, Bristol and Birmingham, with Ryde and Gloucester added later. A joint service with Spartan used Heston as the London airport before moving to Gatwick in 1936. Before the outbreak of war, services were also operated from Croydon to Dieppe and Le Touquet. At one stage, the Southern approached Imperial Airways to acquire its European services, but this was rejected.

► The railways were prominent in the development of air services within the British Isles, and the Southern was more active than most. Typical of the aircraft used was this de Havilland Dragon Rapide. (*LMS Magazine*)

►► An 'H15' hauls a down 'Ocean Liner Express' through Clapham Junction. These trains were scheduled to connect with the major ocean liners. In the late 1930s, carriages for flying-boat passengers were attached to a Bournemouth train as far as Southampton, giving the train the unofficial title of the 'Flying Boat Train'. (HMRS)

In July 1935, Bungalow Town Halt on the line from Brighton to Portsmouth, which had been closed when the line was electrified in 1933, was reopened as Shoreham Airport Halt, with the airport now being used by RAS. From 1936, the Southern station at Tinsley Green served Gatwick Airport, with a tunnel leading to the terminus, known as the Beehive. The station serving Gatwick racecourse was developed post-war to become today's airport station.

During the mid-1930s, the Southern acquired an option to purchase land at Lullingstone in Kent, above the railway tunnel at Eynsford, with a view to developing it as a new airport for London. In 1937 Imperial Airways put this proposal to a House of Commons committee, but towards the end of the Second World War, what is now London Heathrow was chosen instead, despite there being no railway line close to the site. The Southern had no intention of developing or operating Lullingstone, but expected to hand it over to the state so that it could be developed 'like roads'.

Despite competing with road transport and replacing the long-distance stage and mail coaches, the railways needed road transport to take passengers to and from stations, and to collect and deliver goods traffic. At Grouping, many of the vehicles were horse drawn, but between 1929 and 1933, the number of lorries and motor vans operated by the Southern rose from 278 vehicles to 757. With the tremendous growth in road transport after the First World War, the railways felt that road transport had an unfair advantage as it did not have the heavy fixed costs that the railways had.

From 1929, the railways were allowed to buy or invest in bus operators or road haulage firms. In the case of bus services, their own operations had to be sold to established operators, so the Southern and other railways sometimes used their existing services and vehicles as their payment for a share of an established company.

The railways were quicker to move into bus operation than road haulage. Even though the Southern was outside the collaborative collection and delivery operations that the other three companies had developed outside London, it did join the other members of the Big Four in 1933 when they jointly acquired Carter Patterson, the parcels specialist, and Pickfords, the removals specialist. One reason for operating jointly was the fragmented nature of road haulage, with few haulage operators having a nationwide presence.

Once allowed to invest in bus companies, the Southern moved quickly so that by 1930, the company announced that it had acquired the Isle of Wight operator Dodson, which traded as Vectis and was re-registered as Southern Vectis, while

Did You Know?

Away from London, most of the Big Four railway companies combined their goods collection and delivery services to save money while continuing to provide an efficient service. The exception was the Southern, mainly because the company carried relatively little freight in peacetime – apart from coal – but also because, except in parts of the West Country such as Exeter and Plymouth, there was little overlap between the Southern and other companies.

the National Steam Omnibus concern's interests in Dorset had been acquired and registered as Southern National. Other companies in which the Southern had taken a stake included Aldershot & District, the Devon General Omnibus & Touring Company, East Kent Road Car, Hants & Dorset Motor Services, Maidstone & District Motor Services, Southdown Motor Services, Thames Valley Traction and Wilts & Dorset Motor Services.

In many of these areas joint committees were established to coordinate railway and bus services, but, strangely, little attempt was made to substitute bus services for lightly used railway services.

The Southern's predecessors were not new to war, as the LSWR had carried the bulk of the manpower and horses needed for the Boer War, and all of the previous companies had been run by the Railway Executive Committee during the First World War. None of this could have prepared the company for the Second World War, when it became the most bombed of all the main-line railway companies and yet had to meet the needs of the Royal Navy at Chatham, Portsmouth, Gosport, Portland and Plymouth, as well as at Dover, where the civilian population was largely evacuated to avoid German shelling after the fall of France. The Southern also served the army at Aldershot and on Salisbury Plain, while the south was home to many of the RAF's fighter stations.

There were always two aspects to the story of the railways during the Second World War. The first was the part played by the railways in the war effort, which not only included running special trains for the military, but also putting the railway workshops at the country's disposal, producing guns, vehicles and landing craft, even while many skilled railwaymen of all grades had joined the armed forces. The second was the operation of the railways under attack, and the Southern, because of its proximity to German air bases in France, suffered more in this respect than any other railway.

As with the other railway companies the Southern was privately owned during the Second World War, but it was controlled by the Railway Executive Committee (REC). The REC at first introduced speed restrictions and cut the frequency of services; journey times also lengthened. Eventually, the speed restrictions were eased, and public

➤ As with the other companies, many Southern ships were 'taken up from trade' in naval terms. This is the *Isle of Jersey* as a hospital ship. (NRM)

▶ Portsmouth Harbour Station was close to the Royal Dockyard and used by service personnel as well as travellers to the Isle of Wight and Gosport. It was hit by bombs, leaving trains in the station cut off from the rest of the network for the remainder of the war. (NRM)

Did You Know?

Wartime encouraged the Southern to increase the passenger capacity of its suburban rolling stock. One way was to insert an extra carriage into the three-carriage 3 SUB units, making the 4 SUB. Another was to develop a lightweight version of the 4 SUB class with thinner carriage sides, able to carry passengers six abreast.

protest caused the reduced frequencies to be suspended until new ones could be decided on. First class was withdrawn in the London suburban area, and many trains lost their catering facilities, although these were never completely eliminated on the Southern. Pullman carriages were withdrawn and the vehicles put into storage.

The Southern played a leading role in moving the British Expeditionary Force to France, and in bringing it back again with French and other Allied troops after Dunkirk. At the same time that it was busy moving troops to the Channel ports and across to France, the Southern was also playing its part in the evacuation of children and expectant and nursing mothers away from London, the Medway area, Southampton, Portsmouth and Gosport, so that from 1 to 4 September 1939, only a skeleton service could be provided outside the rush hours. In all, seventy-five trains were provided for evacuees in the London area alone for each of the four days, and a total of more than 138,000 children and adults were moved; another 127 trains over the four days took 30,000 people from the Medway and Hampshire ports. Ambulance trains were also provided for the partial evacuation of hospitals.

NEW SOUTHERN RAILWAY
"MERCHANT NAVY" CLASS LOCOMOTIVE
"CHANNEL PACKET"

◄◄ When the Second World War broke out, the shortage of modern goods locomotives on the passenger-orientated Southern was a problem, so the utility 'Q1' class was rushed into production and service. This is preserved No 33001. (Cody Images)

◄ One unexpected arrival during the Second World War was the Southern's first Pacific locomotives, the Merchant Navy class. The first was *Channel Packet*, named after the company's own shipping operations. She was more streamlined than the rest of the Bulleid Pacifics. (Cody Images)

On 11 September drastic cuts were imposed by the REC on train services, imposing great hardship on passengers. Many large companies had dispersed, but not all could do so, and commuter volumes were still almost at pre-war levels. Suburban lines had frequencies cut by a third, while Sunday services were hourly, and a number of services were cancelled completely. Public pressure forced the normal service pattern to be reinstated on weekdays from 18 September. This was only a temporary measure, however, and a revised timetable followed on 16 October.

Main-line services, such as that to Portsmouth, lost their hourly service and had a train every two hours, with additional stops included for 'fast' trains. The Brighton line had just three trains an hour. Cannon Street was closed off-peak on weekdays and all day on Sundays.

By the time of Dunkirk, six of the company's cross-Channel packets and the *Isle of Guernsey* were already taken up as hospital ships, with two, *Maid of Kent* and *Brighton*, bombed and sunk. Another eight, including the *Autocarrier* and the train ferries, were in service as transports. At noon on 29 May 1940 came the order that 'all available Southern steamers of 1,000 tons gross with a range of 150 miles are required for immediate government service'. A further nine ships were handed over, including four Isle of Wight ferries. On 30 May two more ships were sunk and another, the *Paris*, on 2 June.

Ashore, the Southern also played its part, cutting normal services to make as many trains available for the troops. This caused particular problems for the steam-hauled

Did You Know?

Post-war, Oliver Bulleid built two four-car double-deck units which operated out of Charing Cross from 1950 onwards. There wasn't really an upper deck as such, as each upper compartment was reached through the adjoining lower compartment via a set of stairs, so loading and unloading was slow.

◄ More typical of the Bulleid Pacifics in appearance was the Battle of Britain class, such as *257 Squadron*, seen here after nationalisation. Both the Battle of Britain and West Country classes could take boat trains into Southampton Docks, but the Merchant Navy class was too heavy for the dockside lines. (Cody Images)

services, as these had to take the brunt of the work because electric trains could not reach the Channel ports. The Southern also had to handle trains from other companies, with fifty-five trains of its own; forty from the GWR; forty-four from the LMS; and forty-seven from the LNER. In the confusion, drivers were told to 'stop at Guildford and ask where you are going to'. In all, 338,000 men were evacuated.

Britain's railways were reinforced during the war years by locomotives sent by the United States. This preserved example of an 0-6-0T has been painted green, but they would have been black. Note the slight cutaway to the leading ends of the tanks, which improved visibility from the cab. (Cody Images)

At the same time, the Southern was expected to handle a further evacuation of children from the south-east as this area was now within reach of German bombers.

At Redhill, a bottleneck in the system developed, where trains had to reverse to reach the Midlands and the West, more than 300 tons of ash was accumulated

and the station nearly ran out of water for locomotives.

After Dunkirk came the Battle of Britain, as the Luftwaffe tried to destroy the RAF and its fighter airfields. This was followed by the Blitz. Between 24 August 1940 and 10 May 1941 there were raids on the Southern for 250 out of 252 days. Waterloo had to be closed after a bomb caused severe damage to the approaches on 7 September and could not be partially reopened until 19 September. The bomb damage was especially severe and difficult to repair because so many of the lines from the south ran over viaducts to the Southern's London termini. Worst affected were the lines between Queens Road and Waterloo, with more than ninety bombs dropped over 2¼ miles and hardly a line unaffected. On the approach across the Thames to Charing Cross, a landmine fell on Hungerford Bridge, welded to the third rail but failed to explode, while incendiary bombs set fire to Charing Cross itself. Downstream, the approaches to Blackfriars Station were closed when the bridge across Southwark Street was destroyed.

The Waterloo & City Line was closed because of flooding between 8 December 1940 and 3 March 1941, and twice bombs hit the line at the Waterloo end. Fortunately, it was closed due to the flooding on the evening of 11 January 1941 when a bomb penetrated the road surface at Bank Station and fifty-nine people were killed.

The final raid on the night of 10/11 May 1941 saw Waterloo badly damaged by bombs, while incendiaries infiltrated a spirits store in the arches under the terminus. A disused tunnel at Brighton was used to store rolling stock at night, while the Southern had some 'reverse commuters' leaving London to seek shelter in caves at Chislehurst in Kent. At Dover, heavy shelling saw the population drop by more than half.

Bomb damage was not confined to London. On 19 June 1940 bombs destroyed the engineering works at Redbridge, near Southampton. Both Portsmouth & Southsea and Portsmouth Harbour Stations suffered severe damage, and on the night of 11/12 January 1941, the latter was cut off from the rest of the network for the remainder of the war because of heavy bombing. A mine also sunk the Portsmouth–Ryde paddle steamer *Portsdown*, on 20 September 1940, with the loss of eight members of crew and twelve passengers.

Power supplies were affected when power stations were damaged, but as the Southern collected most of its power from the National Grid, there was no serious disruption, and out on the line, electric train services were no more vulnerable to disruption than those of steam trains.

◀ This is what the American tank engines would have looked like in British service. The very different front end and smokebox door gives the game away, showing that this is not a standard British locomotive. They were modified to run on Britain's railways with their much tighter loading gauge. (Cody Images)

In all, the Southern had 170 incidents per 100 route miles, compared to just 33 on the GWR, 29 on the LMS and 28 on the LNER. Due to its proximity to Luftwaffe bases, the Southern had to suffer strafing attacks by fighters, especially in the Dover and Deal areas. At Bramley, one attack badly damaged a Guildford–Horsham train full of civilians, killing seven passengers and wounding everyone but the fireman. The railway was also the victim of many V-1 and V-2 flying bomb attacks, with bridges and power lines destroyed; the worst loss of life occurred when a V-2 hit a block of flats provided by the company for its employees and their families, destroying a quarter of the flats and killing fifty-nine people.

Did You Know?

Before States Airport opened on Jersey, Channel Islands Airways used the beach as a runway. The railways regarded this as unorthodox, yet eventually the Southern Railway and the GWR each invested in the airline. Their misgivings were justified, however, as on one occasion the motor coach used as a booking office and waiting room failed to start as the tide came in and was overwhelmed by the advancing waters.

1) Waterloo was Britain's largest railway terminus.
2) Waterloo was the first railway terminus in the world to be designed for electric trains when it was rebuilt between 1910 and 1920.
3) The Waterloo & City Line was the only genuine tube railway to be operated by any of the main-line companies.
4) The Southern had the most all-Pullman expresses of any railway company, including the 'Bournemouth Belle', 'Golden Arrow' and 'Brighton Belle', the world's first all-Pullman electric multiple unit train.
5) The Southern was the only one of the Big Four companies not to have water troughs, which allowed steam locomotives to pick up water without stopping.
6) The Southern was the only company to operate a through international sleeping car service with its London–Paris 'Night Ferry'.
7) The Southern opened the first two airport stations at Gatwick and Shoreham.

BY DAY!

THE FAMOUS

"GOLDEN ARROW" PULLMAN SERVICE

BETWEEN

LONDON AND PARIS

Via

DOVER-CALAIS SHORT SEA ROUTE

Daily (Suns. included) in each direction

Sea crossing by S.R. Steamer "INVICTA"
Comfortable Private Cabins and Cabines-de-Luxe

BY NIGHT!

COMMENCING DECEMBER 1st, 1947,

Re-introduction of THROUGH SLEEPING CAR
SERVICE, LONDON to PARIS (via Train Ferry)
DOVER-DUNKERQUE ROUTE

Ferry Steamers:
"HAMPTON FERRY"
"SHEPPERTON FERRY"
"TWICKENHAM FERRY"

Entirely reconditioned and redecorated throughout

*SLEEP YOUR WAY TO PARIS—NO CHANGE
EN ROUTE*

For Time-table of Services, Tickets, Reservations, etc., apply to
CONTINENTAL ENQUIRY OFFICE, Southern Railway,
VICTORIA STATION, LONDON, S.W.1,
or Travel Agencies.

Post-war optimism as the Southern advertised the return of the 'Night Ferry' and the 'Golden Arrow', although the former was delayed until a fortnight before nationalisation by an industrial dispute on the French railways. (Southern Railway)

Nationalisation meant a re-evaluation of all the newest steam locomotive classes inherited from the Grouped companies. The Bulleid Pacifics were rebuilt to improve reliability, even though they were economical engines. This is West Country-class *Taw Valley* in preservation. (Cody Images)

◄ Also rebuilt was the Merchant Navy class, including *Clan Line*, seen here after being preserved. Rebuilt, the Bulleid Pacifics were still handsome locomotives, and this image gives a fine impression of power. (Cody Images)

➤ Merchant Navy-class *Canadian Pacific* with an express. Even after nationalisation the then Southern Region largely retained the green livery, even for steam-hauled carriages, but the BR standard 'strawberries and cream' was not unknown and can be seen on the second carriage. (Cody Images)

1834   London & Southampton Railway receives parliamentary approval and is soon renamed the London & South Western Railway (LSWR).

1836   South Eastern Railway (SER) is formed.

1846   London, Brighton & South Coast Railway (LB&SCR) is created by the amalgamation of the London & Brighton and London & Croydon Railways.

1859   London, Chatham & Dover Railway (LC&DR) is formed on the renaming of the East Kent Railway.

1898   Waterloo & City Line opens and is acquired by the LSWR in 1907.

1899   South Eastern & Chatham Railway Companies Managing Committee (SECR) is formed, bringing an end to rivalry between the LC&DR and SER.

1909   LB&SCR electrifies the South London Line, which runs between London Bridge and Victoria using a 6,700-volt DC overhead system.

1910   The rebuilding of Waterloo Station starts.

1912   Herbert Ashcombe Walker joins the LSWR as its last general manager, moving from the London & North Western Railway (LNWR).

1914   The First World War starts and the government takes control of the railways, which remain in private ownership but are administered by the Railway

◄ A late 1930s advertisement by the Southern Railway in Bradshaw clearly demonstrates the pride the company felt in its achievements, with the 'World's Largest Suburban Electric System', 'The Key to the Continent' and the 'magnificent Southampton Docks'. (Bradshaw)

▲ A maker's plate for the SECR. These were affixed to each locomotive with their own production number, similar to a motor vehicle having a chassis number. The main locomotive works for the SECR was at Ashford in Kent. (Cody Images)

◄ The front end of an LB&SCR suburban multiple unit with the pantograph down. Confusingly, the LB&SCR called its electrification system the 'elevated electrics'. (HMRS)

SOUTHERN 105

◄◄ The Southern was the last of the Big Four to receive 4-6-2 Pacific steam locomotives, partly because of its emphasis on electrification and partly because of limitations on its infrastructure, including turntables. Nevertheless, it did have some fine locomotive classes, and the Schools class was Britain's most powerful 4-4-0 class. This is *Tonbridge*. (Cody Images)

◄ A more modest locomotive was this 'U'-class goods locomotive seen in British Railways livery. It is preserved on the Watercress Line, as the Mid-Hants Railway is more usually known. (Cody Images)

Executive Committee. Walker is acting chairman of the committee and is knighted for his service.

1915   LSWR initiates third rail electric services between Waterloo and Wimbledon.

1920   The rebuilding of Waterloo is completed.

1921   Government control of the railways ends. The Railways Act requires the formation of the Southern; Western; North West, Midland and West Scottish; and North Eastern, Eastern and East Scottish Railways.

1923   Southern Railway comes into being.

1925   Former LSWR suburban electrification is completed with the electrification of the Guildford 'new' line from Waterloo via Cobham.

1926   SR announces that it is standardising on third rail for all future electrification and that the former LB&SCR overhead lines will be converted to third rail.

1929   Railway Passenger Duty is abolished on the condition that the sums saved will be capitalised and used for modernisation. Railways are allowed to buy road transport companies.

1930   Suburban electrification is completed, with the third rail reaching Windsor and Gravesend Central.

Most enthusiasts would prefer to see the railway like this, especially as West Country-class *Blackmore Vale* has been preserved in full Southern livery and has not been rebuilt. (Cody Images)

1932   Electric services begin on the Brighton line with six trains an hour off-peak.

1933   The London Passenger Transport Board (LPTB) is formed, and all receipts minus expenses by railways in the LPTB area are pooled, with the Southern allowed a 25.5 per cent share in recognition of its large suburban traffic.

1937   'Portsmouth No 1 Electrification': the Portsmouth direct line, Waterloo to Portsmouth Harbour via Guildford, is electrified.

1938   'Portsmouth No 2 Electrification': Victoria to Portsmouth via Arundel and Chichester is electrified.

1939   The Second World War starts and the government takes control of the railways, which remain in private ownership but are administered by the Railway Executive Committee.

1946   The railways are returned to the control of the Big Four companies.

1947   The Transport Act sets up the British Transport Commission, preparing for the nationalisation of the four Grouped railways, as well as railway-owned ports and road transport.

1948   The Southern is nationalised and becomes British Railways, Southern Region.

BOOKS

Allen, Cecil J., *Salute to the Southern*, Ian Allan, 1974

Dendy Marshall, C.F., *A History of the Southern Railway*, Southern Railway Company, 1936

Klapper, Charles F., *Sir Herbert Walker's Southern Railway*, Ian Allan, 1973

Moody, G.T., *Southern Electric 1909–1979*, Ian Allan, 1979

Wragg, D., *Southern Railway Handbook 1923–1947*, Haynes, 2011

WEBSITES

Isle of Wight Steam Railway: www.iwsteamrailway.co.uk

Mid-Hants Railway/Watercress Line: www.watercressline.co.uk

National Railway Museum: www.nrm.org.uk

Science Museum: www.sciencemuseum.org.uk

The Bluebell Line: www.bluebell-railway.co.uk

Other titles available in this series

ISBN 978 07524 8806 6

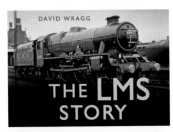

ISBN 978 07524 8805 9

ISBN 978 07524 5914 1

ISBN 978 07524 5604 1

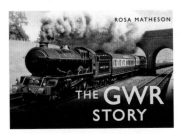

ISBN 978 07524 5624 9

ISBN 978 07524 5084 1